Days That Changed the World

THE FALL OF THE

BERLIN WALL

Jeremy Smith

WORLD ALMANAC® LIBRARY

Please visit our web site at: www.worldalmanaclibrary.com
For a free color catalog describing World Almanac® Library's
list of high-quality books and multimedia programs,
call 1-800-848-2928 (USA) or 1-800-387-3178 (Canada).
World Almanac® Library's fax: (414) 332-3567.

Library of Congress Cataloging-in-Publication Data available upon request from publisher.
Fax (414) 336-0157 for the attention of the Publishing Records Department.

ISBN 0-8368-5569-8 (lib. bdg.)
ISBN 0-8368-5576-0 (soft cover)

This North American edition first published in 2004 by
World Almanac® Library
330 West Olive Street, Suite 100
Milwaukee, WI 53212 USA

This U.S. edition copyright © 2004 by World Almanac® Library. Original edition copyright © 2003 by ticktock
Entertainment Ltd. First published in Great Britain in 2003 by ticktock Media Ltd., Unit 2, Orchard Business
Centre, North Farm Road, Tunbridge Wells, Kent TN2 3XF. Additional end matter copyright © 2004 by
World Almanac® Library.

We would like to thank: Tall Tree Ltd, Lizzy Bacon, and Ed Simkins for their assistance.

World Almanac® Library editor: Carol Ryback
World Almanac® Library cover design: Steve Schraenkler

Photo Credits:
t=top, b=bottom, c=center, l=left, r=right, OFC=outside front cover
Alamy: 9br, 42bl. CORBIS: 1, 4(both), 5, 7t, 8, 10-11, 12, 13, 15, 16, 16-17,
 18, 19, 21t, 26cl, 28t, 29t, 29b, 30t, 30-31, 32, 36, 37, 38-39, 42c.
Hulton Archive: 14, 20-21, 25b, 43t. PA Photos: 22(both), 24.

Printed in the USA

1 2 3 4 5 6 7 8 9 08 07 06 05 04

CONTENTS

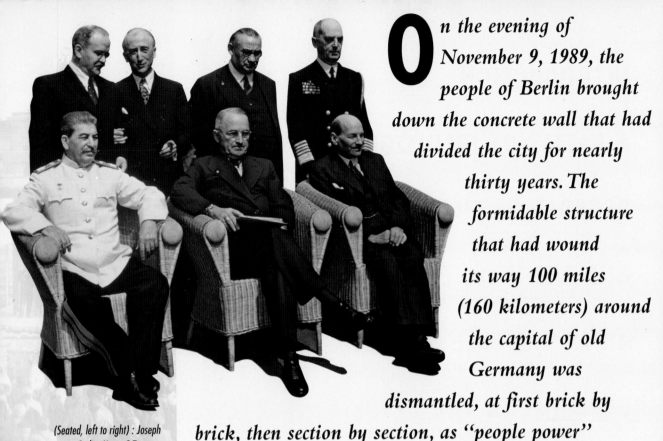

*O*n the evening of November 9, 1989, the people of Berlin brought down the concrete wall that had divided the city for nearly thirty years. The formidable structure that had wound its way 100 miles (160 kilometers) around the capital of old Germany was dismantled, at first brick by brick, then section by section, as "people power" overcame the political divide of East and West.

(Seated, left to right) : Joseph Stalin, Harry S Truman, and Clement Attlee met in Potsdam, Germany, in 1945 to determine the future of Germany after World War II.

Checkpoint Charlie in Berlin was one of the few points along the Wall where people could pass from one half of the city to the other — if they carried the correct documents.

The reasons behind the building of the Berlin Wall date back more than fifty years, to the aftermath of World War II.

After the defeat of Hitler's forces, the victorious Allies divided Germany among themselves. Three of the Allied powers — Britain, France, and the United States — merged their sectors into the country known as West Germany. The Soviet Union claimed the eastern portion of the country and renamed its zone of control East Germany.

However, the question of how to divide the old Germany's historic capital, Berlin, created a problem. Situated more than 80 miles (128 km) inside Soviet East Germany, Berlin was split into two, just like the rest of Germany. West Berlin was governed by a capitalistic system, in stark contrast to the communist rule of East Berlin.

Despite this agreement (and a barrier erected by the Soviets in 1952), the free, prosperous lifestyle of West Berlin lured thousands of East Berlin citizens into West Berlin annually. People simply left the

eastern portion of the city, re-registered as West German citizens, and then escaped to the West.

Security forces struggled to control crowds on the evening the Wall came down.

On the night of August 13, 1961, communist authorities began building the Berlin Wall in an attempt to stem the tide of emigration to the West. Soon a solid concrete barrier replaced the barbed wire ring that ran through the city and created a Wall that split families apart for decades.

French zone
U.S. zone
British zone
Soviet zone

West Germany

East Germany

• Berlin

The Allies divided Germany into two countries after WWII.

INTRODUCTION

Mikhail Gorbachev's election as head of the Soviet Union in the 1980s heralded a period of change which led to the dissolution of the Soviet Union.

Over a period of several decades, hundreds of East Germans lost their lives when border guards gunned them down during attempts to vault over, dig under, or smash through the monstrous wall. As time passed, resentment grew on both sides of the Wall. Slowly, the relationship between the United States and the Soviet Union thawed, and the election of younger, reformist leaders such as Soviet leader Mikhail Gorbachev made the purpose for the Wall seem less certain. The worsening economic situation in East Germany also forced its leaders to make human-rights concessions in return for economic aid. Among other changes, East German leader Eric Honecker suspended the "shoot-to-kill" policy at the Wall during important state visits.

By the late 1980s, communist rule in Europe began collapsing. Hungary dismantled its border with Austria, offering East Germans another escape route into the West. Then in June 1989, the Polish head of state, General Wojciech Jaruzelski, was forced to lift the ban on Solidarity, the workers' union. In Poland's first election in over thirty years, Solidarity stormed to victory. Tadeusz Mazowiecki was elected as head of

6

Eastern Europe's first non-communist government. East Germans started to flood into Poland through foreign embassies, pressuring the East German authorities to make changes. The Wall seemed somehow less frightening than it had before. By 1989, the people of Berlin felt ready to challenge its legitimacy.

After the Wall fell, changes continued in the political landscape of Europe. Romania, Czechoslovakia, and Hungary ousted their communist governments from power. Then — at midnight on October 3rd, 1990 — Germany was reunited. A year later, the communist government in the Soviet Union disbanded, bringing an end to the Cold War and the divisions between East and West.

In the 1990s, Germany's new parliament convened in an impressive building with a glass ceiling that aimed to reflect the new transparency of the nation's political system.

In the more than ten years since Germany's reunification, the benefits and problems for its citizens have become more clear. While the eastern portion of the country remains much poorer than the western sector, the nation as a whole has begun to make its mark both in Europe and the world. Germany is one of the strongest supporters of the single European currency, the euro. It has also played a role in military operations in Kosovo and Afghanistan. Whatever the future holds, after the fall of the Berlin Wall, a reunited Germany remains optimistic about what lies ahead.

Jubilant Berliners climbed on top of the Wall to celebrate its upcoming demolition.

The reasons for the construction of the Berlin Wall go back to the beginning of the twentieth century. In 1917, the establishment of the world's first communist government in Russia (later the Soviet Union) led to increasingly strained relations with the capitalist West. Tensions increased as the victorious Allies debated over how to divide Germany after World War II. Negotiations ended in an agreement that split Germany and its capital into East and West. However, when residents started pouring out of East Germany into the more prosperous West, communist authorities decided to take action. Their response built the Berlin Wall.

Germans Karl Marx and Friedrich Engels developed the ideology of communism.

Capitalism

Capitalism emphasizes the importance of individual rights, and the power of every person to rise by his or her own efforts and merits. Instead of believing that everyone is equal financially, capitalism creates opportunities that rewards individuals who develop ideas for making money. Most western economies are based on capitalism.

Communism

By the early twentieth century, a new ideology called communism thrived throughout parts of Europe. Based on *The Communist Manifesto*, written by Germans Karl Marx and Friedrich Engels and published in 1847, communism put forth a new philosophy that supposedly created a society of total equality. In a communist society, the government controlled all possessions, and all citizens shared equally in the nation's wealth.

The Russian Revolution

Communism carried a strong appeal in countries such as the Soviet Union, where the rich hoarded incredible wealth and the poor struggled to feed themselves. In 1917, a group of revolutionary communists ousted the Russian royal family. Led by Vladimir Lenin, the communists brutally killed Czar Nicholas and his family, and formed the Union of Soviet Socialist Republics (the Soviet Union), the world's first communist state. Joseph Stalin, a more aggressive leader who replaced Lenin in 1928, began spreading communism well beyond the borders of the Soviet Union.

STALIN'S empire

Stalin established an iron grip on the Soviet Union through systematic terror. Between 1934 and 1938, a massive purge known as the "Red Terror" resulted in the disappearance and death of about three million Soviets. Millions of other Soviets were sent to work in labor camps, also known as "*gulags*."

A FRUSTRATED *Germany*

One of the chief causes of World War I and the subsequent rise of Adolf Hitler was Germany's desire to expand its territory. Envious of the money Britain made from its empire, Germany embarked on an ambitious navy-building program. Although Germany's efforts to take European territory were defeated in World War I, its desire remained unquenched. Germany's aggression surfaced again with Hitler's return to power in the 1930s. This time, Hitler hoped to unite the German-speaking people of the world under one "fatherland." But eventually Hitler's ambitions went far beyond this original aim, and his troops invaded countries without any connection to Germany.

Great cities such as New York (right) and London thrive thanks to the capitalistic system.

Germany and the rise of Hitler

The Allies imposed an extremely harsh punishment on Germany after its defeat in World War I (1914–1918). They stripped Germany of most of its wealth and ordered the country to pay compensation, called reparations, to the countries harmed during the conflict. This policy created enormous poverty in Germany, as well as great anger among its citizens — who felt they were being punished too greatly for the mistakes made by their leaders. To make matters worse, disastrous economic policies led to rampant inflation during the 1920s and early 1930s, when people found that a week's wages barely covered the cost of living. Responding to this desperation, the German dictator Adolf Hitler swept to power, promising to restore Germany to its former greatness. Hitler abolished all other political parties, expanded his own power, and introduced a series of racist laws against the Jews — whom he blamed for

most of Germany's problems. Despite Hitler's radical policy on Jews, the majority of Germans — seduced by his charismatic speeches — backed him. Hitler's desire to increase German territory led to Germany's invasion of Czechoslovakia in 1938–1939, and its invasion of Poland in 1939. The invasion of Poland on September 1, 1939, prompted Britain and France to declare war on Germany two days later, on September 3, 1939. World War II had begun.

Adolf Hitler came to power in Germany with bold promises to revive the country's fortunes and increase its influence by expanding its territory.

PROPAGANDA *techniques*

Propaganda involves the spreading of ideas to promote or attack a cause. Stalin used propaganda as a tool to gain the backing of the people. He used the media to convince the Soviet and East German people of the dangers of capitalism, and to persuade them that the Soviet Union was a strong, healthy nation capable of defeating this enemy. Posters, paintings, and literature depicted the Soviet Union as a place filled with fit and happy citizens, and covered up the fact that Stalin sent millions of people who opposed him to their deaths during his reign.

> "The death of a single individual is a tragedy. The death of a million is a statistic."
>
> — Stalin justifies his harsh governmental policies

The Nazi-Soviet Pact

In 1939, Germany and the Soviet Union signed the Nazi-Soviet Pact. Under the terms of this agreement, both countries promised to remain neutral if either country became involved in a conflict. Two years later, despite the Pact, the two nations were at war with each other. In 1941, the Germans invaded the Soviet Union and inflicted terrible damage on the country. Relations between the Soviets and the West also soured during this time because Stalin believed that the Allies had deliberately diverted the Nazis away from Western Europe and into the Soviet Union. Stalin's Red Army eventually drove back Hitler's troops, and Germany found itself under attack from all directions. Forced to retreat to Berlin, Hitler's army was surrounded by U.S., British, and Soviet troops. Germany had little choice but to surrender.

A clash of directions

When World War II ended, the victorious Allies had to decide what to do with the ruins of postwar Europe. The February 1945 Yalta Conference in the Ukraine reestablished the nations destroyed by Hitler during the war. It also carved Germany into four parts — one each for Britain, France, the United States, and the Soviet Union. In July, under the Potsdam Agreement, Germany was again made to pay for the atrocities that occurred under the Nazis. Each of the Allies could take money or goods from their part of Germany. One issue remained — how to split the city of Berlin among the Allies.

Berlin — the oasis

Situated in Soviet East Germany, Germany's capital presented a problem for Britain, France, and the United States. They didn't want to give up their rights in Berlin, but they were also wary of upsetting Stalin, because his Red Army massively outnumbered Allied forces stationed in Berlin. More than one million Soviet troops marched into the German capital in 1945, dwarfing the Allies'

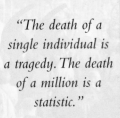

On October 6, 1949, Germany's Soviet sector became the German Democratic Republic (East Germany), and the three Western powers merged their territories to create the Federal Republic of Germany (West Germany). One issue remained: How to deal with Berlin.

Map labels:
- Berlin
- East Germany
- West Germany
- French zone
- U.S. zone
- British zone
- Soviet zone

fifty thousand soldiers. To solve the problem, the Allies divided Berlin into four zones in the same fashion as Germany itself. In 1948, Britain, France, and the United States merged their areas together into a sector called West Berlin.

Stalin's plans

While the western powers made their plans, Stalin began rebuilding the Soviet sector of Germany's capital as a socialist republic. The government controlled all economic activity and used the media in East Berlin and East Germany as a propaganda tool. The state censored daily newspapers and dictated what the East Berliners should think and what views they should hold. This was in stark contrast to the free flow of information

coming from the west of the city, where nearly twenty daily newspapers offering differing political views circulated.

Iron Curtain

The Soviet Union lost more people — twenty million soldiers and civilians — during World War II than any other nation. Consequently, the West held great sympathy for the Soviet Union. Stalin played on these feelings to gain Western approval for his idea that the Soviet sphere of influence should govern Eastern Europe.

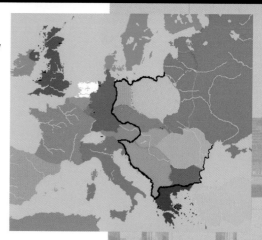

After the end of World War II, the Soviet Union expanded its influence in Eastern Europe. The black line above shows the boundary of the "Iron Curtain." The Soviets ruled countries east of the Iron Curtain. Yugoslavia fell under the Iron Curtain because — despite the fact that it was neither under Soviet control nor a member of the Warsaw pact — communists sympathetic to the Soviet Union's world view held power in Yugoslavia.

After their victory, the Allies gathered at Yalta in the Ukraine to discuss the future of Europe. They agreed to restore countries such as Poland and Czechoslovakia, and to divide Germany among Britain, France, the United States, and the Soviet Union.

NATO *and the Warsaw Pact*

As relations between East and West worsened in 1949, the United States, Canada, and ten Western European nations arranged a guarantee of mutual defense and assistance called the North Atlantic Treaty Organization (NATO). In response, on May 1, 1955, the Soviet Union announced the birth of the Warsaw Pact, a treaty that bound the Eastern communist dictatorships into a single political and military force.

A BATTLE OF IDEOLOGIES

Allied leaders (below) gathered
at the Potsdam Conference.
Seated (right to left): Soviet Premier
Joseph Stalin; U.S. President
Harry S Truman; Great Britain
Prime Minister Clement Attlee.
Standing (left to right):
Admiral William Leahy,
Chief of Staff to President Truman;
the Honorable Ernest Bevin, Britain's
Foreign Minister; U.S. Secretary of State
James F. Byrnes; and the Soviet Union's
Foreign Minister, Vyacheslav Molotov.

HUNGARY *crushed*

In 1956, Hungary's newly appointed prime minister Imre Nagy announced his country's neutrality and withdrawal from the Warsaw Pact. However, the new Soviet leader, Nikita Khrushchev, decided to "make an example" of Hungary. Two hundred thousand Soviet troops invaded Hungary and brutally crushed the rebellion. Nagy sought asylum at the Yugoslavian Embassy, but was captured. The Soviets executed him two years later.

To combat any future threat from Germany, Stalin ensured that Poland, Hungary, Romania, and Czechoslovakia — liberated from Nazism by the Red Army — converted to communism. This new area of influence became known as the "Soviet Bloc." Its boundaries formed the "Iron Curtain" that separated the communist East from Western Europe.

The Truman Doctrine and the Marshall Plan

Leaders in the United States hoped to limit the spread of territory held by the Soviet Union even as it accepted the latter's power of influence in Eastern Europe. Two programs were set up to help contain communism. In 1947, the United States announced a plan called the Truman Doctrine, designed to help countries struggling for freedom against their oppressors. In the Doctrine, President Truman committed the U.S. to assisting any country that felt its freedom infringed upon by another country. The U.S. followed up with the Marshall Plan, an ambitious program of economic aid. By pumping in massive amounts of money to help poor nations recover from WWII, the Marshall Plan would help prevent more countries from coming under the future control of the Soviets. The Marshall Plan enjoyed almost immediate success when U.S. money prevented Italy from turning communist.

The impoverished East

After their division, the two sides of Berlin drifted further and further apart. West Germany and West Berlin turned their gaze completely to the Western world, eventually joining the Council of Europe, the European Coal and Steel Community, NATO, and the European Union. By contrast, Soviet East Germany and East Berlin became more isolated. Living standards slipped and people lined up to buy basic food and supplies.

Berlin Blockade

As West Germany began to thrive, a growing number of East Germans began making their way to prosperous West Berlin to escape from the Soviet East. The situation became even worse when Britain, the U.S., and France introduced a currency called the deutsche mark (DM) into West Berlin in 1948, which made West Berlin an economically attractive place to live. This enraged Stalin, and on March 20, 1948, the Soviet Union declared that it no longer recognized the Allied Control Council of Berlin. Stalin wanted complete Soviet control of the Berlin territory. He closed highways and blocked railroad service that led from Western Germany through Eastern Germany and into West Berlin. The "Berlin Blockade" began in the middle of 1948 when Soviet forces surrounded the Berlin territory in an attempt to starve West Berlin into submission.

The Berlin Airlift

The Allies responded to the Berlin Blockade with a dramatic and daring rescue plan called the "Berlin Airlift." On June 21, 1948, U.S. and British planes began flying food and fuel into West Berlin twenty-four hours a day. When the Soviets saw that the Allies did not intend to abandon Berlin, and lost hope that it would surrender, they offered the citizens of West Berlin food and provisions in an attempt to bribe them into coming over to the eastern portion of the city. That move failed, and in May 1949, the Soviets admitted defeat.

East and West Germany

In 1949, Britain, France, and the United States merged their zones of occupation to create a new country called the Federal Republic of Germany (West Germany). In response, the Soviet Union announced the formation of the German Democratic Republic (East Germany). The first Chancellor of the Federal Republic, Konrad Adenauer, refused to formally acknowledge the existence of East Germany, and relations between East and West deteriorated.

The brain drain

In 1949, the number of East Berliners escaping to West Berlin reached two thousand per week. After the death of Stalin in 1953, it soared to

"I believe it must be the policy of the United States to support free peoples who are resisting attempted subjugation by armed minorities or by outside pressures."

— President Truman stated his intentions in the Truman Plan

The Berlin Airlift dropped a total of 1.2 million tons (1.08 million tonnes) of supplies during the Berlin Blockade. Cargo included coal, food, medical supplies, steamrollers, power-plant machinery, soap, and newsprint.

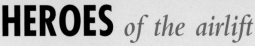

HEROES *of the airlift*

Berlin Airlift missions were extremely dangerous. Planes took off and landed every ninety seconds, and pilots had only about one hour and forty minutes to get their planes refueled, inspected, and ready for a return flight. Pilot Bill Voigt flew to Berlin 116 times between July and November 1948.

"You'd come in at a pretty steep angle. It's not a heck of a lot of space with a fully loaded airplane." said Voigt. Another pilot, Ken Herman, remembered that "when the weather was good you could see as many as six airplanes in front of you." Accuracy was crucial, because if a pilot missed his approach, he had to turn around and take his cargo back to where he came from. Incredibly, during the blockade, there were just thirty-one fatalities in a little under two hundred thousand flights.

THE FOUR *walls*

The "Berlin Wall" ended up as a series of four walls made of different materials. The first was hastily erected the night of August 13, 1961, and made of a mixture of barbed wire, concrete, and square blocks. In June 1962, East Berlin rebuilt it as a stronger wall of reinforced concrete. The third wall, begun in 1965, was even stronger and made of concrete slabs held between steel girders. In 1975, construction of the final wall, made of a new type of impenetrable concrete, began.

Work on the Berlin Wall began at night. In a short time, the original barbed wire fence was torn down and replaced with a solid brick barrier (below).

a staggering six thousand people per week. Although the border between East and West Germany closed in 1952, East Germans still escaped by traveling to the refugee center in Marienfelde, West Berlin. There, they had a choice: either stay in West Berlin or catch a flight to another part of West Germany. Walter Ulbricht, East Berlin's leader, was alarmed that East Germany was losing the equivalent of a small town every year through West Berlin. He convinced Soviet leader Nikita Khrushchev that it was time for drastic action.

Tension at Vienna

In June 1961, Khrushchev met with U.S. President John F. Kennedy in Vienna, Austria.

Khrushchev threatened that unless the Allies agreed to certain terms, he would force Allied troops out of West Berlin and seize total control of the city. Kennedy was furious and insisted that any action against West Berlin "would result in war." Two years later, in June 1963, Kennedy flew to West Berlin to show his support for its residents, and declared *"Ich bin ein Berliner"* ("I am a Berliner").

The plan is hatched

After the 1961 Vienna meeting failed to reach an agreement regarding the East Berlin refugees flooding into West Berlin, Ulbricht met secretly with Soviet leaders at the Kremlin in Moscow. In a confidential memo from Erich Honecker (the future leader of East Germany), plans were

raßensperrung
verursacht durch die
Schandmauer

made to erect a physical barrier between East and West Berlin. By the evening of August 12, 1961, rumors circulated about a plan to divide the city. Trains that ran east failed to return, and Berlin's *Schnellbahn* ("fast train") system — also called the *S-Bahn* — ground to a halt. West Berlin taxi drivers began refusing fares to the eastern portion of the city, and tourists visiting the historic Brandenburg Gate that night were refused access.

Building the Wall

Early on the morning of August 13, 1961, the East German government began blocking off the eastern part of Berlin. Barbed wire marked the barrier at first. Soon afterwards, East German troops forced some citizens of East Berlin at gunpoint to help erect a concrete barrier. Troops also evacuated houses along the dividing line. If residents did not leave by the time specified, soldiers threatened to brick up the houses with the people still inside. On August 23, 1961, East German officials warned West Berlin citizens that they could not enter East Berlin without a permit, and if they did enter, they were to stay for good. The Soviets responded to criticism by referring to the new barrier as an "anti-fascist protection wall."

Walled In

What became known as the "Berlin Wall" divided at least sixty major roads. It crossed graveyards and railway stations — and even cut through the middle of one house. East Germany demolished

factories, apartment blocks, and anything else that got in the way of the Wall's path. The barrier even disrupted Berlin's famous *S-Bahn* train system. More than three hundred watchtowers guarded a north-to-south vacant strip of land that separated the Wall from the rest of East Germany — all to prevent people from leaving East Berlin.

Checkpoint Charlie

Nine days after the Wall went up, East Germany began preventing people from Britain, the United States, and France from gaining access to East Berlin. The East Germans closed five checkpoints between the two halves of the city, one of which was the sector-crossing point at Friedrichstrasse. On September 22, 1961, the United States set up a new checkpoint near Friedrichstrasse. It became known as "Checkpoint Charlie" and, until 1990, served as the only crossing point for non-Germans between East and West Berlin.

Checkpoint Charlie was a potential flash point where East came directly into contact with West. A white line painted across the road signified exactly where the influence of the United States and their Allies ended.

The Berlin Wall stretched for almost 100 miles (160 km) around the entire border of West Berlin. An amazing 66 miles (106 km) of the concrete barrier towered 13 feet (4 m) high. More than three hundred watchtowers, twenty bunkers, and twelve checkpoints guarded the Berlin Wall. On the night the wall came down, people from both sides swarmed the seven checkpoints that separated West and East Berlin.
1. Bornholmer Strasse
2. Chausseestrasse
3. Invaliden Strasse
4. Checkpoint Charlie
5. Heinrich-Heine-Strasse
6. Oberbaumbrücke
7. Sonnenallee

It took the people of Berlin many years to adjust to the Wall, and some never came to terms with the divide. Sadly, the Wall is famous for the numbers who lost their lives trying to scramble over, dig under, and find other ways to breach it. By the end of the 1960s, however, the political landscape of the world was changing, and the future of the Berlin Wall looked less certain.

East German guards carry away the lifeless body of Peter Fechter.

August 1961

In August 1961, as the barbed-wire barriers were being replaced with a brick wall, people burrowed under houses on the Wall's border to escape, wriggling through tunnels to the sanctuary of the West. East German Rudolf Urban was attempting to cross the divide through a house in Bernauer Strasse when workmen began bricking up the doors and windows. Urban's friend got out in time, but Urban fell from a window and broke his ankle. He was taken to an East German hospital for examination, but mysteriously, he was later reported dead. By the end of August, the East German authorities had hardened their attitudes towards attempted escapes, and "shoot-to-kill" was the policy at the Wall's border. Houses adjacent to the Wall became popular escape routes. On October 4, 1961, student Bernard Lanser jumped from the roof of a house near the Wall, but landed awkwardly. Border guards gunned down Lanser, and beat to death the man who was helping him flee. Eventually, the authorities ordered residents closest to the wall to move away. East Germans needed to come up with ever more cunning ways to outsmart the border guards. One 33-year-old East German rented an American soldier's outfit from a costume shop in East Berlin and managed to walk through Checkpoint Charlie unnoticed.

PETER *Fechter*

Peter Fechter was the most famous casualty of the Berlin Wall. The eighteen-year-old and his friend climbed over the wall from a building in Zimmerstrasse. Fechter's friend made it over, but Fechter was shot. He collapsed back onto the eastern side, just 167 feet (50 m) from freedom. Fechter bled to death before the authorities took his body away.

Another used a high-powered sports car with the windshield removed to race under the barbed-wire barriers. Other escapees resorted to less refined methods. A group of East Germans used a truck reinforced with steel and concrete to ram through a checkpoint in front of bewildered guards.

Cold War Showdown

In spring of 1961, a failed invasion, or coup, to overthrow the government of communist leader

VIETNAM

The Vietnam War was a battle between the U.S.-backed Republic of Vietnam in the south, and the Communist Democratic Republic of Vietnam in the north. The war lasted from the mid-1950s until 1973, when U.S. troops withdrew. South Vietnam surrendered in 1975. The Vietnam War was important in relation to the Cold War because it made the United States realize that it could not stop the spread of communism. Discussion and negotiation with the East — rather than military aggression — was the best course of action.

Fidel Castro at Cuba's *Bahia de los Chochinos* ("The Bay of Pigs") increased tensions between Cuba and the United States. But the real showdown of the "Cold War" came in October 1962 during the "Cuban Missile Crisis." Photographs taken by a U.S. spy plane flying over Cuba revealed several military bases capable of firing Soviet-supplied nuclear missiles at the United States. Castro hated the United States and U.S. President John F. Kennedy. Likewise, Kennedy distrusted Castro. Kennedy placed a naval blockade around Cuba, which forced the Soviets to withdraw their missiles. In return, the U.S. promised never to invade Cuba. Kennedy and Soviet Premier Khrushchev also set up a special telephone connection between the two countries to prevent a war from beginning by mistake. In August 1963, both countries signed the nuclear test-ban treaty.

January 1968

In January 1968, Alexander Dubcek was elected as the new leader of Czechoslovakia. During what became known as the "Prague Spring," Dubcek announced a series of reforms that included the abolition of censorship and the right of Czech citizens to criticize their government.

Fidel Castro is so revered in Cuba that his full name is hardly ever mentioned in public — most people call him "Fidel" or simply touch their chin to indicate his flowing beard. When Castro, then aged 32, and his comrades swept to power in Cuba on January 1, 1959, he became the youngest leader on the planet. Castro eventually adopted the communistic ways of government and depended heavily on the Soviet Union for trade, including gas and oil supplies. Castro made enemies in the United States when he took control of several U.S. corporations located in his island nation without paying for them.

DECADES OF CHANGE

Over the next four months, Dubcek worked hard to convince the Soviet Union's leaders that Czechoslovakia planned to remain within the Soviet Bloc and would not return to capitalism. Despite these assurances, the Soviet Union invaded Czechoslovakia on August 20, 1968. In contrast to the Soviet invasion of Hungary twelve years earlier, the troops entering Czechoslovakia did not meet armed resistance, but instead faced jeering crowds who showed no warmth towards their communist masters.

1971 Willy Brandt, chancellor of West Germany developed a policy called "*Ostpolitik*" to improve relations between the East and West. *Ostpolitik* led to the "Basic Treaty." In it, the Federal Republic of Germany and German Democratic Republic agreed to develop normal relations and recognize each other's borders. Under *Ostpolitik*, the Federal Republic of Germany also exchanged ambassadors with the Soviet Union, Poland, Czechoslovakia, Hungary, and Bulgaria.

1972 Relations between the United States and the Soviet Union improved dramatically. Both superpowers met at the SALT (Strategic Arms Limitation Talks) Conference to discuss production limits of nuclear missiles. The Helsinki Accord, which contained important human rights legislation, followed the SALT talks. Another SALT meeting was planned for 1979. However, on Christmas Day, 1979, the Soviet Union invaded Afghanistan. In protest, the U.S. suspended talks and refused to send athletes to or participate in the 1980 Olympic Games in Moscow.

1978 Despite its earlier pledge to remain independent from the West, the East German government acknowledged that it needed help from capitalistic countries to fight off poverty. Erich Honecker, the East German leader, agreed to the implementation of human rights reforms in return for economic aid from West Germany. East Germany also dismantled guns along its western border because of two large loans.

By the 1970s, the United States and the Soviet Union had stockpiled hundreds of nuclear weapons between them. Just a few of these weapons could wipe out most life on Earth.

A SUPERPOWER *no more*

In 1983, U.S. President Ronald Reagan announced plans for the Strategic Defense Initiative, or SDI, a nuclear-defense program capable of destroying enemy missiles in space before they reached their target. SDI made the Soviet Union realize that it could not afford to match U.S. defense plans. Then in 1988, a rebel force (aided by the U.S.) called the *mujahedin* drove Soviet forces out of Afghanistan. The Soviet Union's status as a superpower began to disintegrate.

WALL ART *on the western side*

During the 1980s, many artists started to paint the western side of the Wall. In stark contrast, however, the eastern side of the Wall remained untouched. Graffiti artists knew they risked being shot if they entered the strip of no-man's-land to reach the Wall. However, after its collapse in 1989, artists finally began to make their mark on the eastern side of the Wall. Only a few painted sections of the former Berlin Wall remain, but a gallery with a permanent display of Wall art has been established.

> "Mr. Gorbachev, tear down this wall!"
>
> — U.S. President Ronald Reagan challenges Gorbachev to end the division of Berlin in 1987

1981 Former movie actor Ronald Reagan won the U.S. presidential election. Naturally suspicious of the Soviet Union, Reagan vowed to get tough with what he referred to as "the evil empire." However, Reagan's advisors urged him to adopt a more peaceful relationship with the Soviet Union. This appealed to Reagan because he saw arms reduction as a way of saving money, and it would allow him to make good his campaign promise of tax cuts for U.S. citizens.

1982 Helmut Kohl became Chancellor of the Federal Republic of Germany in October, 1982. A confident man, he refused to keep apologizing for Germany's past actions. Instead, he encouraged the people of his country to look to the future. Kohl was the driving force behind later plans for German reunification and, along with President François Mitterrand of France, for greater unity in Europe.

1985 In 1985, Mikhail Gorbachev was elected as the Soviet Union's new leader. Gorbachev introduced new ideas — such as *Glasnost* (greater freedom of speech) and *Perestroika* (economic reform to allow profit-making)

— into Soviet politics. Gorbachev firmly believed that change "was knocking at every door and window," and that "life punishes those who come too late." While previous Soviet leaders responded with bullets and tanks, Gorbachev's willingness to talk and deal with situations calmly helped end the Cold War. Gorbachev allowed a clutch of countries to leave the Soviet Bloc peacefully (*see pages 20–21*), and respected the right of individuals to choose their own destiny. On October 7, 1989, Gorbachev urged Erich Honecker to enact reforms in East Germany, and appealed for "brave decisions" from him.

Born after the Russian Revolution, Mikhail Gorbachev was a relatively young man when he was elected as the new leader of the Soviet Union in 1984. Raisa, his glamorous wife, loved to dress in Western clothes.

Austria became a haven for East Germans after it opened its borders with Hungary.

May 1989 In May 1989, communist Hungary made the momentous decision to dismantle its wire border with Austria. For years a favorite destination for East German vacationers, the opening up of Hungary enabled tens of thousands to escape to the West. Anyone wanting to leave the communist East could now simply travel to the Hungarian border, disappear into the woodlands, and scurry across the border to Austria. From there, they could continue to West Germany, where they automatically became citizens of the democratic nation. By the end of September, an incredible thirty thousand East Berliners escaped to freedom through Hungary.

August 1989 Other residents headed for the Federal Republic's consulate in East Berlin. On August 8, the consulate closed because the number of refugees turning up at its doors spiraled out of control. When this happened, people headed instead for the FRG's consulate in Budapest, Hungary; as a result, this also closed. Later, refugees swamped the FRG Embassy in Prague, Czechoslovakia, and were authorized to emigrate by the Czech government.

June 1988 Erich Honecker was, for many years, unrepentant about the hundreds of people killed trying to escape to the West. He expressed regret only for his "twenty-five comrades who have been treacherously murdered at the border" — guards killed by escapees in self-defense. Honecker suspended the shoot-to-kill policy at the Wall during special state occasions, but tragically, the deaths continued. On February 5, 1989, Chris Gueffroy, a twenty-year-old waiter, was the last to be shot by border guards. His death provoked a storm of international outrage, but it also marked a moment of true change: Gueffroy's family was allowed to place a funeral notice in East German newspapers, something that had never happened before. Western media attended the funeral and published photographs of the event across the world.

June 1989 Developments elsewhere in communist Europe reflected the mood for change in East Germany. In 1988, the ruling Communist Party in Poland faced a wave of labor strikes that economically crippled the country. By June 1989, the Polish head of state, General Wojciech Jaruzelski, lifted the ban on the workers' union, Solidarity, and called for free elections. In Poland's first election in more than over thirty years, Solidarity stormed to victory. Tadeusz Mazowiecki was elected as Eastern Europe's first non-communist leader.

LEIPZIG *church*

Local elections held in East Germany on May 7, 1989, provoked more unrest. Allegations of vote-rigging began. Protesters made their way to the Nikolai Church in Leipzig, where a crowd of 20,000 marched to Karl Marx Square. Amazingly, the military took no action against the protesters.

October 1989 Gorbachev's plans to visit East Berlin for the fortieth anniversary celebrations of East Germany's founding frightened East Berlin's rulers. Fearing a mass demonstration on the Western side of the city against Gorbachev's presence, the border guards began erecting a new, reinforced wall at Checkpoint Charlie. When Gorbachev arrived in the German capital on that hot October day in 1989, demonstrators on the streets of East Berlin greeted him, pleading, "Gorby, help us! Gorby, help us." In the Western side of the city, angry crowds pelted border guards with bottles and eggs. After Gorbachev left Berlin, the new wall at Checkpoint Charlie was torn down, but the political mood had changed forever. Protesters had been allowed to demonstrate without the threat of violent repression. Erich Honecker, a hardened opponent of Gorbachev's reforms, declared that "the Wall will still be standing in fifty or one hundred years if the reasons for its existence are not removed." But his beliefs were becoming increasingly outdated. On October 18, 1989, Honecker was deposed by reformers in his own party. Egon Krenz replaced Honecker and inherited a country which

East German leader Erich Honecker and his wife, Margot, held fast to communistic ideals. Honecker's opposition to any discussion about demolishing the Berlin Wall made him increasingly unpopular.

was virtually bankrupt. Instead of using the weapon of fear to force citizens to stay in Berlin, he pleaded with his people: "Your place is here. We need you." To appease the increasing number of demonstrators, the *Politburo* announced that starting on November 1, 1989, East Germans would be allowed to travel to the West for a maximum of thirty days.

During a visit from Pope John Paul II, Polish demonstrators gathered to protest the banning of the Solidarity trade union. Although the Polish government made Solidarity illegal from 1981 to 1989, it became a national movement backed by the Roman Catholic Church in Poland.

THE NEW FORUM *movement*

After Hungary opened its borders, a handful of East German activists formed a group called the New Forum. The group aired views on East German reform during weekly meetings and radio broadcasts. It also created a manifesto for reform.

AND THE WALL CAME DOWN

A CRITICAL SITUATION

At midnight on November 9, 1989, an incredible eleven thousand East Germans fled to West Germany via Czechoslovakia. A vast tide of people flooded the Western embassies in Prague, from where they could re-register as West German citizens. Alarmed at the scale of the exodus, the Krenz government called a press conference to announce a new travel law to help address the problem.

East Berlin Party Secretary Gunter Schabowski made the momentous announcement.

*B*y November 1989, the divisions between East and West Germany were already fragmenting. On the night of November 9, the wall started to crumble. Following a speech by a government official named Gunter Schabowski, border restrictions were effectively lifted, and people began to make their way in the thousands towards the checkpoints.

THE CHOSEN MAN

Around 5:40 P.M., the East Berlin Party Secretary, Gunter Schabowski, met with Prime Minister Krenz to discuss the press conference scheduled for 6:00 P.M. Krenz gave Schabowski a document with the new travel law written on it, and said, "Announce this. It will be a bombshell." Flustered by recent events, however, Schabowski failed to read the script properly.

THE CONFERENCE BEGINS

At the end of the news conference, Schabowski announced that East Germany was lifting all travel restrictions. "Private trips abroad can be applied for without questions, and … the People's Police have been instructed to hand out long-term exit visas without delay." A journalist asked Schabowski when the new regulation would take effect. He stammered, "As far as I know, this enters into force ... this is immediately, without delay."Schabowski was questioned again by a journalist and he repeated that "permanent emigration can take place at all GDR border crossing points to the Federal Republic and West Berlin." It is unlikely that Schabowski realized what he just said. When he was asked by a journalist later if the law would lead to mass emigration, he replied, "I hope it doesn't come to that."

Schabowski was visibly nervous after the news conference.

NEWSFLASHES

Just four minutes after Schabowski finished his speech, the world's major news agencies began sending frantic newsflashes around the globe. While Reuters announced the new travel arrangements, the Associated Press agency went much further, speculating that the borders would be coming down immediately.

VIEWPOINT

"We had no warning of what he was going to say, although we thought something might happen. We made up our minds we had understood it correctly, and that he had opened the wall: we replayed a video of it just to make sure. And then, of course, everybody was very busy writing, and writing, and writing."

— Journalist Erdmute Greis-Behrendt reaction to Schabowski's speech

"A young man... was waving at us. 'Hey folks, you know what? The borders are open! Isn't this weird?!' How can this work, I ask myself. Will we be the last ones to turn out the light in the GDR then? Will everyone go west now that it shall be so easy? This sounds so incredible that I can hardly grasp it."

— East German Thomas Khalou's reaction to Schabowski's speech

BORNHOLMER STRASSE CHECKPOINT — 19:05

While the world's media had already decided about the fate of Berlin's Wall, passport officials in East Berlin remained skeptical. Harald Jaeger, the man in charge of passport control at the Bornholmer Strasse checkpoint, refused to accept that Schabowski had made anything other than a mistake. "What does this Schabowski mean by 'immediately'? That is simply not possible."

Officials at Bornholmer Strasse refused to believe the announcement.

AND THE WALL CAME DOWN

VIEWPOINT

> "Looking around I saw an indescribable joy in people's faces. It was the end of the government telling people what not to do, it was the end of the Wall, the end of the war and of East and West."
>
> — an East German recounts his elation

> "I am just so happy. Berlin is Berlin again! Now finally this hated wall has been smashed down and we can be together again. I have friends and family in the East that I haven't seen for years."
>
> — Jurgen Schwarker from West Berlin

THE NEWS ON THE NEWS   `19:30`

The German television channel ZDF broadcast the news of Schabowski's speech at 7:17 P.M., as the sixth story of the night. At 7:30 P.M., the GDR program *Aktuelle Kamera* reported the event as its second item; word started to spread. Then the 8:00 P.M. broadcast on West Germany's ARD evening news reported that the border was completely open.

BORNHOLMER STRASSE   `20:00`

By the time Schabowski's speech was broadcast on national television, the number of people gathering at Bornholmer Strasse had grown from a steady trickle to a deluge. By 8:30 P.M., thousands surged around the checkpoint, because — unlike Checkpoint Charlie — Bornholmer Strasse was located in a busy residential area.

Lines began forming at the Bornholmer Strasse checkpoint within an hour of the announcement.

PRESSURE BUILDS 21:00

By 9:00 P.M., the crowd had grown to tens of thousands. A line of cars snaked down the main road and spilled over onto the side streets as well. Harald Jaeger, the head of passport control, was instructed by his headquarters to let any troublemakers pass through. The officials planned to stamp identity cards so that the residents would not be able to return to East Berlin. By 9:20 P.M., several hundred East Berliners had already passed through the three passport huts at the border into West Berlin. Meanwhile, the crowds left behind chanted "Open the gates, open the gates."

Crowds jostle for the best viewpoint at Bornholmer Strasse.

CHECKPOINT CHARLIE 21:30

At the same time that people were massing at Bornholmer Strasse, a crowd of a few hundred gathered on the western side of Checkpoint Charlie. They urged the guards to let the people on the other side come through into West Berlin, but were politely refused. By 10:00 P.M., a few people stepped out of the crowd and stepped over the dividing line, technically crossing onto East German territory. They were gently pushed back by border guards, who were still being told by the authorities that there were no changes to the status of the wall.

People in West Berlin test the resolve of border guards at Checkpoint Charlie.

25

VIEWPOINT

> *"Everything was out of control. Police on horses watched, powerless."*
> — Rainer Pterck, a visitor to Berlin, describes the scenes

> *"I just can't believe it! I don't feel like I'm in prison anymore!"*
> — Angelika Wache, 34, the first visitor across Checkpoint Charlie

> *"Go have a beer."*
> — a West Berliner to Torsten Ryl, one of many who came over just to see what the West was like, as he hands Ryl a 20-mark bill (worth about $11.50)

WE CAN'T HOLD FOR MUCH LONGER

22:45

The ARD's nightly news announced that "the gates in the Wall are open," despite the fact that the checkpoints were still physically shut. Pressure at the border crossings became unbearable, and guards had an extremely difficult time keeping order in the increasingly restless crowds.

UP ON THE WALL

22:50

At Checkpoint Charlie, the attitudes of the guards changed visibly. Bewildered by the excitement, they disobeyed an order to close the pedestrian gate at Checkpoint Charlie. People began streaming toward the Wall, and started climbing onto it. Major Bernie Godek of the U.S. Army recorded that "People were sitting on the wall with their legs draped down, almost lolled, casual as you like." As this was happening, many of the guards removed their helmets and joined the sea of people pressing up against the Wall — some even even agreed to take photographs for West Germans.

Guards at many of the checkpoints were buckling under the pressure (above).

People began climbing onto the Wall at various checkpoints.

Bornholmer Strasse was one of the first checkpoints to open.

CHECKPOINT CHARLIE

00 : 00

At Checkpoint Charlie, East German commander Gunter Moll faced a baying crowd from both directions. In East Berlin, the crowd shouted, "Let us go! Let us go!," while in West Berlin, thousands urged, "Come! Come! Come!" At one minute to midnight, Moll decided to open the pedestrian gate.

ONE OF THE FIRST

23 : 00

n East Berlin, the pressure continued to build. A crowd of about twenty thousand people pressed up against Bornholmer Strasse checkpoint, encouraged by news that the Rudower Chaussee checkpoint in the south of the city had opened. A noisy chant of "Open it! Open it!" began. As Harald Jaeger realized he danger of holding back such a huge number of people, he gave the order to "Open them all." These three words unleashed a jubilant torrent of people from East o West. At 11:35 P.M., the Heinrich-Heine-Strasse checkpoint further south was also opened.

People poured through Checkpoint Charlie at midnight.

AND THE WALL CAME DOWN

10·11·89

As the new day arrived, people began celebrating with bewildered border guards.

CHECKPOINT CHARLIE

00:50

All the border guards had abandoned their posts by midnight and began to mingle with the crowd. Realizing that they had lost control and that what they thought they had been protecting just didn't matter any more, they threw away their guns. Overcome by the joyous atmosphere, they celebrated the freedom of the city with the other revelers. Drinks passed freely through the crowd, and for the first time in twenty-eight years, no one cared what side of Berlin they came from: They were all Berliners — and nothing else mattered.

BORNHOLMER STRASSE

01:35

The thousands amassed at Bornholmer Strasse let out a roar and started going through, as well as up and over, the checkpoint and the Wall. West Berliners pulled East Berliners to the top of the barrier where, in years past, people trying to cross over had been shot. At 1:35 A.M., Chris Toft of the British Military Police reported that people "were chipping away at the Wall with hammers." These would soon be replaced with bulldozers.

Angry Berliners began chipping away at the wall.

VIEWPOINT

"Over 20,000 East and West Germans were gathered in a huge party ... Between lanes of cars, a group of musicians were playing violins and accordions, and men and women were dancing in circles."

— East German Gunter Hanski remembers the night the Wall fell

"In front of the Brandenburg Gate, the wall measured four feet across, so there was enough room for hundreds of people to stand and drink. Women beseeched guards: 'Come up here! Drink! Dance! It's all over! Forget the damned wall! Forget the GDR!' I never tired of watching Germans fall into each other's arms."

— Henry Porter in "The Brandenburg Gate Opens"

ANGER IN THE EAST

Huge crowds in Berlin began to celebrate the collapse
of the Wall, hoping that it would unite East and West Germany.
They were also angry at the lies they had been told for years
by their government, and began to demonstrate. Revelers set
fire to cars draped in the East German flag and chanted for
the reunification of Germany. Eventually, the crowds dispersed
as more and more people headed west to the heart of Berlin.
Many East Germans were desperate to meet up with friends and
family on the other side, some of who they had not seen for years.

Many vehicles were destroyed in East Germany as people expressed anger at their government.

BRANDENBURG GATE

Two hours later, visitors from the West had started coming into the other side of Berlin.
Many headed for the Brandenburg Gate, a point right on the dividing line. People climbed
and danced on its wall while guards watched.

FREE MOVEMENT

As dawn broke in Berlin, cars moved freely from
East to West. Many East Germans were returning
home after a giddy night in the West. After years
of having to exist on the most basic food and
supplies, Eastern shoppers loaded up their bags
with fruit, cigarettes, and electrical goods. Many
were simply unable to believe what they found
in the West, where supermarket shelves groaned
with every imaginable luxury. "Going to West
Berlin was as good as going to Australia for me,"
said one East German.

"**D**evelopments are now unforeseeable," said West German Chancellor Helmut Kohl. "The wheel of history is turning faster now." By early 1990, the prospect of reunification became more and more likely. Kohl was becoming increasingly vocal in his demands to unite the countries. Public unrest forced East Germany's prime minister, Hans Modrow, to start thinking about the prospect of one, united Germany.

In December 1989, West German Chancellor Helmut Kohl and East German President Hans Modrow met at Dresden, East Germany, to discuss greater cooperation between the two countries. Barely one year later, the two halves of Germany reunited.

Last remnants

By the evening of November 11, the first concrete slabs were removed. The next day, borders at Potsdamer Platz — once one of the busiest crossroads — were finally flung open. The West Berlin Philharmonic Orchestra marked the event.

Kohl and Gorbachev

Chancellor Helmut Kohl was visiting the Polish Prime Minister in Warsaw when the Berlin Wall came down. As soon as the news about the Wall reached him, he cut short his visit and flew to Berlin for a rally. As Kohl waited to speak, he received a telephone call from the Soviet Ambassador in Berlin, who had a message from Mikhail Gorbachev. The Soviet leader wanted to know if citizens were attacking Soviet bases in East Germany. Realizing that Gorbachev was being fed false information by his political opponents in the Soviet Union who were opposed to any reform, Kohl told an aide to reassure Gorbachev that there was no truth to any of these rumors.

Tourists to the West

After the collapse of the Wall, an estimated two million East Germans visited West Germany. Day passes were issued to anyone wanting to travel to West Berlin, and thousands of people piled onto free trains provided by the West German government. One visitor observed that

TRABI *cars*

When the Wall fell in 1989, West Berliners saw hundreds of odd looking cars puttering out from the east of the city. These plastic-and-fiberglass vehicles were *Trabants*, or "*Trabi*" cars. With a top speed of 62 miles per hour (99 kilometers per hour), and a tiny but noisy engine that sounded more like a motorbike, the *Trabi* seemed hopelessly primitive when compared to Western cars. Today, people remember the cars with affection, and an international meeting for ex-*Trabi* owners attracts thousands of visitors every year.

"more than eighty percent of East Germany was vacationing in West Germany." Universities in East Germany canceled lessons as it soon became apparent that all their students were deserting classes in order to visit the West. Once there, East Berliners could visit any bank and receive 100 DM (about $57 U.S.) of "Welcome Money" — the equivalent of several months wages in the East. West Berlin volunteers offered cakes to the Easterners, thinking they couldn't afford to eat.

Collapse of the Soviet Bloc

The fall of the Berlin Wall set off a ripple that reverberated around Europe. The Communist Party in Czechoslovakia resigned as a result of a mass demonstration on November 17, 1989. In December 1989, former Solidarity leader Lech Walesa was elected president of Poland. In Hungary, the ruling Communist Party dissolved and announced free elections scheduled for March 1990. In Romania, a bloody December revolution occurred in which

SELLING *the Wall*

Within weeks, tourists eagerly snapped up souvenir pieces of the Wall. Stalls operated by East Germans, Poles, and Turks quickly sprung up along the path of the fallen barrier. Tourists wanted painted pieces of Wall sections from the eastern side — so the sellers sprayed them to get a better price. Others bought genuine East German and Soviet army uniforms. Today, it is still possible to purchase Wall fragments, both in Germany and all over the world via the Internet.

the communist dictator, Nicolae Ceausescu, and his wife, Elena, were executed. In less than six months, the Iron Curtain had vanished.

Hans Modrow

Newly elected Prime Minister Modrow caught the mood. He proposed "a community of treaties" to increase cooperation between the two Germanies. However, he believed that East and West Germany should remain two nations, despite the fact that East Germans continued to desert their country and head westwards.

The population in Prague celebrated wildly after hearing that the Czech Communist Party resigned on November 24, 1989.

THE STASI's *reign of terror*

"*Stasi*"was the name for the notorious East German secret police. They arrested political opponents and threw anyone who disagreed with the government's political policies into prison. The full extent of the *Stasi*'s chilling reign of terror become evident when the Berlin Wall was toppled in 1989. As the communist regime collapsed, *Stasi* officials frantically attempted to destroy incriminating documents but were caught before they succeeded.

Reality check

In West Germany, people's attitude towards the *Ossies* (Easterners) began changing as day-to-day reality replaced the jubilation. Millions of East Germans flooded into West Berlin every weekend, and locals found their streets blocked as *Trabant* cars coughed their way down city streets. They also faced long lines at banks behind Easterners waiting to collect their welcome money. Many West Berliners were losing patience with their neighbors. Many East Germans also felt that they had lost their dignity when the Wall went down. One remarked, "I feel like a beggar if I go to take my 100 Marks."

Aid for elections

On November 28, 1989, Helmut Kohl announced for the first time that he wanted to unite the two Germanys. He made an offer to East Germany that West Germany would provide millions of dollars of economic aid in return for free elections in East Berlin.

Chaos

The political situation in East Germany became increasingly unstable as the end of 1989 loomed. Mass emigration continued, and East German money lost its value. Although a few people hoped for an independent East Germany, most East Germans increasingly favored unification.

Victims of the Stasi gather in Leipzig, East Germany, on December 18, 1989. People feared that the hated secret police planned to launch a new crackdown in East Germany, so they held regular demonstrations outside the Stasi building.

THE *Stasi files*

Stasi files revealed that the secret police had a staggering 85,000 full-time employees plus half a million informants who made it their business to find out everything that was going on in East Germany. More than one-third of all East Germans were spied upon by the *Stasi*, and investigators found a massive collection of reports that are still being sifted through. After the fall of the Wall, all Germans were allowed access to their files. Many were astonished to find that family members and close friends had in fact been spying on them. The files also revealed the hypocrisy of East German society. While the ordinary people of communist East Germany lived simple lives with few luxuries, leaders such as Erich Honecker owned lavish hunting lodges complete with servants and staff and took expensive holidays in the West.

The commissioner's archives house in Berlin holds an incredible 76 miles (122 km) of Stasi files. More than 1.7 million Germans have visited the building to inspect their files, and many were shocked at what they found.

Reunification Resistance

Kohl's reunification plans were received with mixed reactions abroad. Britain's Prime Minister Margaret Thatcher was alarmed about the prospect of a united Germany, and wished to "check the German juggernaut." French President Mitterrand was furious. His outrage was understandable, considering Germany's history of invading France. However, Mitterrand was confident that the Soviet Union would never allow it. "I don't have to oppose it — the Soviets will do it for me," he declared. Only the U.S. supported German unification from the start. Although President George H. W. Bush didn't wish to upset the Soviet Union — which suffered greatly at the hands of the Germans— he did not fear the prospect of one, united, Germany.

End of the Stasi

On November 20, 1989, thousands of East Germans marched through Leipzig, chanting, "We are the people." They feared that the ruling party was trying to increase its power — a suspicion that grew when the communists held a large "anti-fascist rally" in January. When Prime Minister Modrow announced plans to replace the hated *Stasi* with a new secret police force, East Germans took action. On January 15, 1990, protesters stormed the *Stasi* headquarters in East Berlin and tore the building apart, daubing the walls with anti-communist slogans.

Kohl meets Gorbachev

Chancellor Kohl knew he needed to persuade Soviet leaders that German reunification would not threaten the Soviet Union. On February 10, 1990, Kohl met with Gorbachev in Moscow, promising that Germany would respect current borders and that Soviet trade with East Germany would continue unaffected. Gorbachev finally saw, "no differences of opinion ... about unity and the people's right to seek it." Kohl flew home triumphant. He announced on German television that the Soviet Union would not oppose unification.

PHYSICAL *symbols removed*

At a startling rate, Berlin removed the physical symbols of division within a few months after the fall of the Wall. Lenin's statue disappeared from Leninplatz, East Berlin. And while a marching band played in the background, a huge crane destroyed the Allied hut at the infamous Checkpoint Charlie.

On the day Germany was finally reunited, hundreds of thousands of East and West Germans massed in the center of Berlin.

Modrow's free elections

On February 1, 1990, East German Prime Minister Hans Modrow decided to support reunification, declaring "the unification of the two German states is now on the agenda." Then, on March 18, East Germany held its first free elections. Most of the parties standing were backed by political groups from the West, including the "Alliance for Germany" party, backed by Kohl himself. The favorites, the Social Democratic Party, or SPD, made several mistakes along the way, including an announcement by a former member that he was "an alternative Marxist." Desperate not to re-elect a communist-style government, voters supported Kohl's party, tempted by his slogan: "Without Kohl, no cash."

Reunification happens

The final step was to draft an agreement to replace an unsigned peace treaty drawn up by the Allies at the end of World War II. On July 16, 1990, Kohl signed an agreement with the Allies called the "Two (Germanys) Plus Four (Allies) Treaty." This treaty ended the Allies' rights in Germany, and allowed the new Germany to remain in NATO, as long as its authority didn't

MORE *celebrations*

Many East and West Germans were completely overwhelmed when it was announced that Germany would again be one nation. One East German woman, Ursula Grosser Dixon, said, 'I completely lost my composure. People were singing the German national anthem in the streets. As tired as I was, I have never enjoyed a celebration more in my life.'

> "The Soviet Union will respect the decision of the Germans to live in one state, and that it is up to the Germans to decide [for] themselves the time and the way to unite."
>
> *Chancellor Kohl*

extend to former East Germany while Soviet troops were still stationed there. These troops would be withdrawn after four years. There was also a commitment by Germany not to obtain a nuclear arsenal. Then at midnight on October 3, 1990, less than eleven months after the Wall came crashing down, Germany was officially reunited.

Bonn or Berlin?

The new German government needed to select a capital. Two options under consideration were Bonn, the capital of the old West Germany, and Berlin, East Germany's capital and Germany's historic first city. Bonn's location was so far from what had been East Germany that the new government decided former East German citizens might feel excluded from the political process. So, in 1991, Berlin became Germany's capital city. Gradually, the government offices and activities were moved from Bonn to Berlin. The move was finally completed in 2000.

War crimes trials

Attention now focused on those who had committed terrible crimes against people attempting to cross the Wall. In September 1991 — despite their pleas that they were only obeying orders — four former border guards were convicted of killing Chris Gueffroy. Former prime minister Erich Honecker was charged with manslaughter because of his "shoot-to-kill" policy, under which 192 people died. Honecker only escaped jail because he was terminally ill. Egon Krenz, who presided over East Germany after Honecker, received a six-and-a-half-year sentence, while Gunter Schabowski served three years in prison.

Egon Krenz, the former prime minister of East Germany, received a six-and-a-half-year prison sentence for his part in the crimes committed during the communist regime.

After reunification, rapid change continued in Germany and in the rest of Europe. Just two years after the fall of the Berlin Wall, the Soviet Union collapsed. A wave of immigrants attracted to a united Germany led to the emergence of Neo-Nazi groups in the old West Germany. Wars in Europe and the Middle East tested the new Germany's foreign policy, even as the fledgling nation played a crucial role in the shaping of a new Europe.

The Reichstag building features a glass-and-steel dome from which visitors can look down into the parliamentary chamber. This design is meant to reflect Germany's commitment to more visible government.

Soviet Union collapses

Gorbachev's policy of allowing countries in the Soviet Bloc to leave peacefully infuriated many communist hard-liners. They began plotting to remove him, and in 1991 seized power in a coup, imprisoning the Soviet leader. Street protests, led by future president Boris Yeltsin, finally ended the coup. Although Gorbachev returned to power for a brief period, his grip had weakened and he resigned on August 24, 1991. Boris Yeltsin replaced Gorbachev in the Soviet Union's first free elections. The Communist Party officially disbanded after that, and in December 1991, the Soviet Union — along with the last remnants of the Cold War — broke up. Yeltsin declared, "The world can sigh again in relief."

Differences and divides

As the years passed, many citizens became disheartened at life in reunited Germany. In former East Germany, about two-thirds of all the senior public- and private-sector jobs were filled by people from the former West. Despite the billions of deutsche Marks pumped into the former East Germany, salaries remained much lower there than those in the western portion of the country. Many former West Germans shared the resentment as former East Germans, willing to work for less money, filled local, low-paying jobs. "Some people say it's a good thing, some people say we should build the Wall back up," said one West German bricklayer, after losing some of his business to East Germans who had moved in and used government aid to undercut prices.

Immigration

Immigrants flocked to the new Germany. With borders flung open all across Europe, the country

GERMANY'S *new parliament*

In June 1991, the *Bundestag* began transferring parliament and government to Berlin. The new parliament and government were to be based in the *Spreebogen*, the area around the old Reichstag building that linked the eastern and western parts of Berlin. The *Reichstag*, the new seat of the German government, was given a new glass dome, and was opened to the public, giving visitors a bird's-eye view of Germany's capital.

attracted more and more immigrants from Eastern Europe and beyond. Reunited Germany had no official immigration laws, so immigrants simply entered as political refugees and hoped the government would grant them asylum. By 1992, Germany was accepting nearly eighty percent of all asylum seekers in Europe.

Neo-Nazis

General unease at the number of people entering Germany exploded after the April 1991 announcement that Poles could enter Germany without visas. Neo-Nazis began blocking border-crossing points, and threw objects at Polish buses and cars. In June, two thousand "skinheads" arrived in Dresden,Germany, giving Nazi salutes while shouting "Heil Hitler!" and *"Auslander raus!"* (Foreigners out!). During the summer of 1992, a number of disturbing attacks on immigrants and asylum seekers were reported in the German media. Germany's

MURDER *in Molln*

On November 23, 1992, two neo-Nazis set fire to a Turkish family's house in a small town called Molln, killing a woman and two girls. The German public was revolted at this violence toward people who had been in Germany for several generations. By the end of January 1993, nearly three million people had protested against the violence.

reputation suffered further when the courts treated these Neo-Nazi thugs leniently.

The Gulf War and Kosovo

Not long after Germany celebrated its unification, the first Gulf War began in January 1991. A pacifist Germany, still wary of military involvement, opted to offer financial support instead of sending troops. By the time the war was over, Germany had contributed about $3 billion (5.3 billion DM) to the war effort. However, just a few years later, Germany actively supported the NATO bombing campaign in Kosovo, and provided troops for the multinational force in 1999.

The popularity of the Far Right soared in the reunited Germany. During 1992 alone, nearly three thousand attacks on immigrants and other outsiders, including the homeless, were recorded as West Germans grew increasingly resentful of supporting their neighbors from the former East Germany.

CLOSING *the past*

By the late 1990s, Germany had paid more than 104 billion DM ($60 billion) in compensation to Hitler's victims. Then, after some high-profile business takeovers in Germany in 1998, Holocaust survivors in the United States filed a series of lawsuits against German companies who had used slave laborers during the war. In December 1999, Schroeder set up a 10 billion DM ($5.7 billion) fund for the families of the former slave laborers.

The charismatic Gerhard Schroeder replaced German leader Helmut Kohl. Schroeder was a professional politician who had previously served as Minister President of the German province of Lower Savoy.

The European Union

After German reunification, Chancellor Kohl and French President Mitterrand began working on an ambitious project to bring Europe closer together. Kohl was determined that Germany should play a key role in this process. The December 1992 treaty signed in Maastricht, Netherlands, committed fourteen European nations to a stronger alliance. At another meeting in the Netherlands in 1997, plans were announced for the launch of a single currency — the euro. Along with France, Germany was the major driving force behind integration. Kohl declared that "the building of the 'United States of Europe' would be 'the major success story of the next century.'"

Kohl voted out of office

On September 11, 1998, Germans voted Helmut Kohl — the driving force behind German reunification — out of office. His popularity slumped as many East Germans began to feel that he was not keeping his promises. Despite the fact that he had put aside billions of deutsche marks to revitalize the east of the country, many felt Kohl had not delivered the "flourishing landscapes" he had promised.

Schroeder's Germany

Gerhard Schroeder, the leader of the SPD, replaced Kohl as Chancellor. A snappy dresser who liked to smoke expensive cigars, the new leader fired the imagination of the German public. Declaring that "the era of Helmut Kohl is over," Schroeder promised a new era for Germany, together with wealth for all. He remained committed to the launch of the euro, but his attitude towards Germany's role in the world changed. Born in 1944, Schroeder was the first German chancellor who was too young to remember World War II, and this had a major effect on his foreign policy.

38

Germany and European defense

Under Schroeder, Germany began to take a more active role on the world stage. About four thousand armed German troops joined peacekeeping forces in Kosovo and Macedonia in 1999. Hoping that such participation might in some way make up for atrocities committed during World War II, Schroeder stated that "German soldiers here are showing a Germany always hoped for in this region but not seen until now." After this peacekeeping role, Germany was also involved in successful operations to remove Afghanistan's Taliban regime in 2001.

Anniversary celebrations

On Tuesday, November 9, 1999, Germany and most of the world stopped to remember the fall of the Wall ten years earlier. Former U.S. President George H. W. Bush, former Soviet leader Mikhail

MEMORIAL *to the Wall*

In August 1998, plans were announced to erect a Wall memorial at the *Bernauer Strasse*. The monument consisted of a 230-foot (70-m) piece of the Berlin Wall with slits cut into it and steel sheets at the end.

Gorbachev, the German Chancellor Gerhard Schroeder and his predecessor, Helmut Kohl, arrived in Berlin for the occasion. Musicians performed on the barren strip where the Wall had stood. Children born as the Wall came down were also invited to come and celebrate their birthdays with Berlin's mayor.

The tenth anniversary celebrations drew tens of thousands of people to the center of Berlin. Festivities included a New Year's Eve laser show by the Brandenburg Gate.

"The day will come when a German would not make an automatic apology every time they entered a room."

Willy Brandt, former chancellor of West Germany, predicts a positive future for Germany

*T*he beginning of the twenty-first century has been an exciting time for Germany. More than ten years after the collapse of the Berlin Wall and the Soviet Bloc, Germany now uses a new currency, the euro, and is at the center of plans for a European army and an international criminal court. Many people in Germany are also hopeful that the gap will continue to narrow between residents of the former East and West. This would result in a truly united and content nation.

Hello euro

On January 1, 2002, Germans replaced their deutsche marks with euros, the brand-new single currency of the European Union (EU). Germany also continued to press for an enlargement of the European Union. In the future, Germany and the other EU members hope that the euro will become a serious rival to the U.S. dollar and help create a more secure and prosperous Europe.

New terrors

Like many Western countries, the main threat to Germany comes not from traditional enemies but rather from terrorist organizations such as al-Qaeda. In the World Trade Center attack on September 11, 2001, many of the terrorists studied in Hamburg, Germany, and formed illegal terrorist cells there. After this shocking event, Chancellor Gerhard Schroeder realized the need to support "international alliances" against the "privatized violence of … terrorists."

Defense

In 2002, Germany and the Netherlands led the International Security Assistance Force (ISAF) in Kabul, Afghanistan. But in 2003, Germany — along with France — chose not to join U.S. and British forces that entered Iraq with the goal of destroying Saddam Hussein's dictatorship. Instead, Germany and France chose to support the force through increased aid to the United Nations.

Germany and France were the two main countries that pushed for a single European currency, the euro. After some initial problems, the currency became accepted. Germany remains the banking center of the new Europe.

GERMANY *and the United Nations*

In 1996, the United Nations (UN) set up several organizations in Bonn, including the United Nations Information Center. On January 1, 2003, Germany became a non-permanent member of the UN Security Council. Germany is also one of more than sixty nations who set up an International Criminal Court (ICC), in which individual criminals from different countries stand trial for "crimes against humanity."

A HEALTHY *economy*

Despite lean times at the beginning of the twenty-first century, Germany's economy remains powerful, and has an annual GDP (Gross Domestic Product) worth about $2 trillion U.S. dollars. Germany leads the world in producing chemicals, steel, machinery, vehicles, and electronics. Many famous brand-names of cars, such as BMW, Mercedes, and Porsche come from Germany. In fact, Germany stands second only to the United States in terms of world trade.

Germany is known for the quality of its manufacturing, particularly its cars. This exotic sports car (left) is made by BMW, a German car company. Other famous models of German cars include Porsche, Volkswagon, and Mercedes-Benz. Germany sells millions of cars all over the world each year.

European Army

In 1991, France, Germany, Spain, Belgium, and Luxembourg created an armed force called Eurocorps, based in Strasbourg, France. This mini-army contained up to sixty thousand troops, and served in Bosnia-Herzegovina and Kosovo. However, Germany proposed the idea of a more permanent European Army to replace national forces. Under the proposals for a rapid reaction force announced in 1999, a new EU force with roughly the same number of troops as Eurocorps, including up to four hundred combat aircraft, will be created. This EU force would be capable of sustaining a military operation for up to one year.

Uniting people

One of the main problems facing Germany after reunification was the lack of economic equality between those living in the East and those in the West. In an effort to bring the two sides together, the government continues to pour huge sums of money into the former East Germany, investing in transportation and communication networks, as well stimulating job growth in small businesses. By 2000, manufacturing companies in the eastern part of Germany grew at a healthy rate, and many believe that by 2005, the former East Germany will catch up economically with the rest of the country.

The Eurofighter Typhoon is a shining example of increasing European military cooperation. Four countries — Germany, Italy, Spain, and Britain — together produce fighter planes that can rival the top U.S.-made models.

1800–1938

- *1848: Publication of Marx and Engels' the* Communist Manifesto. *It becomes very popular in parts of Europe, particularly Russia.*

- *1914: The assassination of Archduke Franz Ferdinand leads to the outbreak of World War I.*

- *1917: Communist revolution topples Russia's Czar Nicholas.*

- ▼ *1933: Hitler and his National Socialist (Nazi) Party elected to power in Germany.*

1939–1946

- *1939: Nazi-Soviet Pact signed in August between Germany and the Soviet Union.*

- *1941: Hitler ignores the 1939 Nazi-Soviet Pact, and his forces storm into the Soviet Union.*

- *December 7, 1941: Japan attacks Pearl Harbor, Hawaii; the U.S. enters World War II.*

- *1945: Yalta Conference held in February to discuss what to do with Germany after World War II ended.*

- *1945: Potsdam Agreement formulated between July 17–August 2 in Potsdam makes Germany pay for its actions during World War II.*

- *1945: The Allies defeat Hitler's troops; U.S. drops atomic bombs on Japan; end of World War II.*

- *1946: Sir Winston Churchill makes "Iron Curtain" speech, declaring that "an iron curtain has descended across the continent" in response to the conversion to communism of Poland, Hungary, and Czechoslovakia.*

1947–1952

- *1947: Truman Doctrine announced in March, followed by the Marshall Plan in June.*

- *1948: Berlin Blockade and Berlin Airlift begin in June. More than one million tons of supplies are delivered to the city, including a gift of a camel called Clarence!*

- *1948: The Soviet Union explodes its first nuclear bomb.*

- *1949: The U.S., Canada, and several European nations form NATO (North Atlantic Treaty Organization); the official formation of the GDR (German Democratic Republic) in East Germany and the FRG (Federal Republic of Germany) in West Germany.*

- *1949: Mao Zedong founds the communist People's Republic of China on October 1.*

1953–1960

- *1953: Stalin, age 74, dies in the Soviet Union.*

- *1955: Warsaw Pact formed. A military alliance of the Eastern European Soviet Bloc countries set up in response to the NATO alliance, its members were the Soviet Union, Albania, Bulgaria, Romania, East Germany, Hungary, Poland, and Czechoslovakia — all the communist countries of Eastern Europe except Yugoslavia.*

- *1955: War begins in Vietnam between the U.S.-supported Republic of Vietnam in the South and the communist Democratic Republic of Vietnam in the North.*

- *1956: November uprising in Hungary is brutally crushed by the Soviet army.*

1961–1970

▲ 1961: Construction of Berlin Wall begins during the night of Sunday, August 13.

• 1962: Cuban Missile Crisis in October. The world comes close to nuclear war as Kennedy and Khrushchev fall out over Soviet missiles stationed in Cuba. The Soviet leader eventually agrees to remove the missiles.

• 1963: Kennedy visits the Berlin Wall on June 26, 1963 and makes his famous "Ich Bin Ein Berliner" speech.

• 1968: Beginning of "Prague Spring" in Czechoslovakia. The reformist leader, Dubcek, is removed when Soviet troops invade the country.

• 1970: Ostpolitik agreement announced by Chancellor Brandt of West Germany. East and West Germany exchange ambassadors for the first time.

1971–1988

• 1972: SALT conference limits arms.

• 1973: U.S. admits defeat in Vietnam and the entire Asian country becomes communistic in 1975.

• 1979: Soviet Union invades Afghanistan. The U.S. immediately abandons promises made at the SALT conferences in response.

• 1981: Ronald Reagan elected president of the U.S.

• 1985: Gorbachev elected leader of the Soviet Union.

1989–1990

• June 1989: Communists lose election in Poland.

• October 1989: Gorbachev visits Berlin and comes face-to-face with protesters appealing to him for help.

• November 1989: Berlin Wall falls on the evening of November 9.

• December 1989: Communist government dissolves in Czechoslovakia; uprising in Romania topples the hated dictator Ceausescu. Free elections announced in Hungary.

• April 1990: Free elections lead to non-communist government in Bulgaria.

• 1990: East and West Germany reunited on October 3.

1991–2004

• 1991: A coup in the Soviet Union removes Gorbachev from power. He is reinstated after protests led by Boris Yelstin, but later replaced by the latter. The Communist Party in the Soviet Union resigns and dissolves itself.

• 1991: Germany commits financial aid, not troops, to first Gulf War.

• 1991: New parliament to be built in Berlin.

• 1992: Maastricht treaty signed.

•1998: Gerhard Schroeder replaces Helmut Kohl as Germany's leader.

• 1999: Germany commits troops to Kosovo.

• 1999: Germany adopts single European currency, linking the deutsche mark to the euro on January 1.

• 1999: The renovated Reichstag, home to Germany's new parliament, opens April 19.

• 2002: Euro replaces deutsche Mark in Germany.

• 2003: Start of second Gulf War; Germany and France opt out.

• 2004: EU welcomes Czech Republic, Cyprus, Estonia, Hungary, Latvia, Lithuania, Malta, Poland, Slovakia, and Slovenia.

airlift the delivery of goods and essential supplies by aircraft.

Allies the countries — the U.S., Britain and the British Commonwealth, the Soviet Union, and France — that fought together against the Nazis and the Japanese during World War II.

asylum seeker a person who flees from persecution or trouble in one country and tries to stay in another country for safety.

Axis the countries — Germany, Italy, and Japan — that fought against the Allies during World War II.

British Commonwealth a group of independent nations that consider Britain the "Motherland," use the British system of government, and honor the Queen of England as a figurehead.

capitalism an economic system that promotes a free market and the rights of an individual to own property and reap financial rewards with as little interference from government as possible.

checkpoint a post on a boundary or border where guards check a person's identification papers before passage to another region.

Cold War the period after World War II which describes the tension — but not an actual war — between the communist countries (led by the Soviet Union) and the capitalist West (led by the U.S.).

communism a political and economic system which exercises strict controls over its citizens, and in which all property is owned and distributed equally by the government.

coup (pronounced "koo"); an overthrow of a government.

currency money

czar title for the Russian ruler up until the 1917 Revolution when Lenin seized control and formed the communistic Soviet Union.

democratic a system of government where all of a country's population has a vote in choosing who runs that nation's government.

deutsche mark the old German currency.

emigration the movement of people from one region to another.

euro the single European currency which replaced the old currencies in many European countries.

fascism a form of government ruled by a strict dictatorship.

GDP (Gross Domestic Product) the amount of money that a country produces each year from all aspects of business and industry.

graffiti drawings, symbols, or words painted on a public surface.

gulag a Soviet prison and labor camp.

Gulf Wars the two Middle East wars, so-called because they occurred near the Persian Gulf. In 1991, the U.S. and coalition forces responded to Iraq's invasion of Kuwait. In 2003, the U.S. and coalition forces removed Iraqi leader Saddam Hussein from power.

Holocaust the term used to describe the genocide, or mass murder, of millions of Europeans — especially Jews — in gas chambers at the hands of the Nazi regime during World War II.

ideologies the theories and ideas of a political system.

immigration the movement of people into a region or country.

inflation an increase in the prices of goods and services while their value remains unchanged.

Iron Curtain the name for the dividing line between capitalistic and communistic countries in Europe. Winston Churchill first used the term in 1946.

juggernaut an overpowering force that destroys everything in its path.

manifesto a written declaration of views, intentions, or motives.

media the organizations responsible for reporting the news.

mujahideen an Islamic "guerilla" fighter who wages a holy war.

NATO (NORTH ATLANTIC TREATY ORGANIZATION)
a coalition of Western countries, including Britain, the U.S., France, and Canada, formed to protect each other against any threats posed by communist countries.

Nazi a member of the National Social German Worker's Party with extreme fascist political views who supported Adolf Hitler's rise to power in the 1930s and upheld Hitler's philosophy of government for Germany.

Neo-Nazi someone who now believes in and supports the political views of the Nazis; a skinhead.

Ostpolitik a policy developed by German chancellor Willy Brandt in the 1960s and 1970s that attempted to improve political relations between West Germany and its communistic neighbors.

peacekeeping force a military force sent into a war-torn region in an attempt to keep the peace.

propaganda the manipulation of news and information in order to convey a particular political message.

purge to cleanse — or get rid of — sometimes by killing.

reunification joining together again of what was once split apart.

SALT (Strategic Arms Limitation Talks) a series of meetings between the political leaders of the U.S. and the Soviet Union regarding agreements about and limits on nuclear weapons.

SDI (Strategic Defense Initiative) also called "Star Wars" — a space-based missile defense system proposed by the U.S. and intended to destroy incoming Soviet nuclear missiles.

shoot-to-kill to shoot people with the intention of killing them rather than just hurting them or scaring them away.

skinheads people who (usually) shave their heads and hold extreme, often violent attitudes — similar to those put forth by the Nazis of World War II — toward anyone who isn't caucasian (white).

soviet the name of a council in a communist country. The term was also used to describe anything or anyone from one of the former communist countries.

Soviet Bloc the name given to the communist countries of Eastern Europe (also called the Eastern Bloc).

Soviet Union (the Union of Soviet Socialist Republics) also known as the USSR, the enormous communist country which was formed by the unification of several regions, including Russia, Latvia, the Ukraine, and Georgia. The Soviet Union broke up in 1991 after the Communist Party lost its power.

Stasi the secret police of East Germany. The *Stasi* collected information and compiled files on people inside their own country, and also carried out kidnappings, and beat and tortured citizens.

Taliban an extreme Islamic group who seized power in Afghanistan and imposed a strict Muslim regime. U.S.-led forces toppled the Taliban when they invaded Afghanistan in 2001.

trade union a group which represents workers from a particular industry and negotiates on their behalf on issues such as wages and working conditions.

vote-rigging the illegal slanting of votes that controls the final outcome of an election.

Warsaw Pact the coalition of former communist countries, including the Soviet Union, Poland, East Germany, and Czechoslovakia, in response to the establishment of NATO by Western countries.

Books

The Berlin Wall. At Issue in History (series). Cindy Mur, Ed. (Greenhaven Press)

Berlin Wall: How It Rose and Why It Fell. Doris M. Epler (Millbrook Press)

The Berlin Wall. New Perspectives (series). R.G. Grant (Raintree/Steck Vaughn)

Cold War: American Crusade Against the Soviet Unon and World Communism, 1945–1990. James A. Warren (Lothrop Lee & Shepard)

The Cold War: Collapse of Communism. History's Great Defeats (series). Earle Rice Jr. (Lucent Books)

The Fall of the Berlin Wall: The Cold War Ends. Point of Impact (series). Nigel Kelly (Heinemann Library)

The Fall of the Berlin Wall. Dates With History (series). Brian Williams, John Malam (Smart Apple Media)

The Fall of the Berlin Wall, November 9, 1889. Days That Shook the World (series). Patricia Levy (Raintree/Steck-Vaughn)

Mercedes and the Chocolate Pilot: A True Story of the Berlin Airlift and the Candy that Dropped From the Sky. Gijsbert Van Frankenhuyzen (Sleeping Bear Press)

Web Sites

www.papaink.org/gallery/home/artist/images/96.html
View the graffiti that decorated the Berlin Wall.

learningcurve.pro.gov.uk/coldwar/
Discover links on the history of the Berlin Wall.

www.pwc.k12.nf.ca/coldwar/plain/cuba.html
Learn about the Cuban Missile Crisis.

history.acusd.edu/gen/20th/coldwar0.html
Study Cold War policies from 1945 to 1991.

www.wall-berlin.org/gb/berlin.htm
Read the history of the Berlin Wall.

www.cubacrisis.net/angl/pages/prem00.html
Explore the turning point of the Cold War.